WINNING AT WORK READINESS

STEP-BY-STEP GUIDE TO

BECOMING A LEADER AT SCHOOL & ON THE JOB

Jeri Freedman

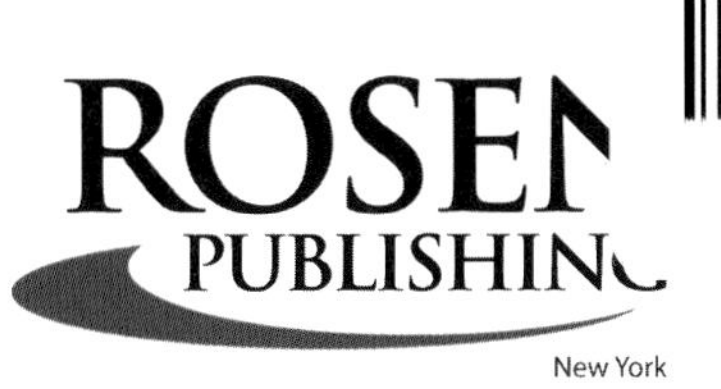

New York

Published in 2015 by The Rosen Publishing Group, Inc.
29 East 21st Street, New York, NY 10010

First Edition

Library of Congress Cataloging-in-Publication Data

Freedman, Jeri.
Step-by-step guide to becoming a leader at school & on the job/Jeri Freedman.—
First edition.
pages cm.—(Winning at work readiness)
Includes bibliographical references and index.
ISBN 978-1-4777-7778-7 (library bound)—ISBN 978-1-4777-7780-0 (pbk.)—
ISBN 978-1-4777-7781-7 (6-pack)
1. Leadership—Juvenile literature. 2. Leadership in children—Juvenile literature.
I. Title. II. Title: Step-by-step guide to becoming a leader at school and on the job.
HM1261.F743 2015
303.3'4—dc23

2014003061

Manufactured in the United States of America

CONTENTS

INTRODUCTION

The world of business and industry is changing. Business has become global, and automation has become widespread. Automation means that there is less need for routine skills. In contrast, globalization means that there is a great demand for skills that can be used to bring diverse people together and make projects successful. According to many business, nonprofit, and education leaders, skills in communication, leadership, and creative problem solving are just as important—if not more important—than academic knowledge. The qualities that make one a good leader, such as having a vision, being able to inspire people, and being an excellent communicator, are critical for success in business today.

People are not born leaders. Even people who appear to be natural leaders were not born that way. Those people developed the skills and the qualities that made them successful. They may have been taught these skills by their parents, picked them up by observation, or learned them from personal experience, but they did learn them. Like them, you can learn the skills necessary to be a good leader. The time to develop these skills is while you are in school. There are many opportunities to develop and use leadership skills in class, team, and community projects.

Developing leadership abilities makes one more successful not only in a work setting but also in any setting where working with others and completing projects is involved. School projects and school clubs; political campaigns; charity events, such as races or walkathons; social action groups, such as SADD (Students Against Drunk Driving) or the Sierra Club; a part-time job;

Student volunteers for Students Against Destructive Decisions host a charity event during the holiday season to raise awareness. Such events allow students to practice leadership skills.

fund-raising activities, such as bake sales or car washes; and neighborhood projects, such as cleaning up a playground, all offer opportunities to learn and practice leadership skills.

Being a leader requires a lot of energy and dedication. One must be willing and able to deal with diverse people and problems. However, being a leader can produce great rewards. It allows people to realize their goals. It makes the leader's groups successful. Developing leadership skills while in school can make one more successful when entering the workforce in the future. Being a leader also allows one to positively affect the lives of others.

Chapter 1

STARTING THE JOURNEY

Before you can become a leader, it's necessary to understand what a leader is. A leader is a person who can motivate a group of people to take the actions necessary to achieve a goal. In some cases, a leader may also be in a position that gives him or her authority over people. The captain of a sports team, the president of the student council, and a manager in a business have authority, but authority alone does not make one a leader. Many people who are leaders do not have any official position. They may belong to a school club or volunteer with a charity organization. Yet these people have qualities that make other people believe in them and their ability to achieve a goal.

WHY BE A LEADER?

Why should someone want to be a leader? Being a leader can be rewarding in both practical and emotional ways. Being a leader while in school can lead to achievements that can be included on a résumé or college application. More important, being a leader allows you to develop practical skills that will help you be successful once you get a job or enter college. Beyond the practical benefits, being a leader puts you in situations where you can develop a positive self-image and enhance your self-confidence. It can also provide the satisfaction of achieving a goal, helping other people develop their talents, and having a positive effect on other people's lives.

WHAT IS LEADERSHIP?

To understand what leadership is, it is necessary to know what it is not. Leadership is not ordering other people around or forcing

The leader of a girls' high school soccer team helps set up the players. Getting the team members to pull together to be successful requires leadership skills.

people to do things. It means getting other people to want to accomplish the tasks that will achieve a goal. This is why it is possible for a person at any level of authority to be a leader. A leader has a vision, or a concept of how things could be. A leader has the commitment and drive to make that vision a reality. A leader doesn't just imagine the way things might be, however. A leader has the ability to organize people and resources so that the vision becomes reality. A leader perseveres and keeps others working toward a goal despite obstacles. Above all, a leader must be articulate—that is, able to communicate clearly and effectively. A leader must be able to describe his or her vision and explain why it is important. He or she must be able to convey to others what their roles are and motivate them to do what is necessary to achieve the group's goal.

IT'S NOT ABOUT YOU

Leadership is not about showing how smart or capable the leader is. It is about making a group of people successful. To accomplish the goals of a group, a leader needs to motivate people, and motivating people requires focusing on others and understanding them.

Running a successful campaign requires understanding what is important to other people and convincing them the candidate can provide it. This ability to understand people is an important leadership skill.

Whether a group is working on a school project or a team project at work, leadership is the art of making people want to perform

ADVICE FOR NEW LEADERS

Global Zero is an organization devoted to a world without nuclear weapons. The following advice from Global Zero is excerpted from the organization's website. It is aimed at student leaders working with Global Zero, but it is excellent advice for student leaders in a wide range of endeavors:

- Collaborate with other student groups: This is a great way to make contacts and spread the word.
- Aim for diversity: People with different opinions, backgrounds, and skills will expand the reach and capacity of your team.
- Go online: Create a Facebook group or your own blog for your group, and get all your members and friends to follow or "like" it.
- Have informational meetings: When someone shows interest, find out what excites him or her about the undertaking, and leave the meeting with a clear plan of action for how he or she can contribute.
- Remind people why the project matters: Organizing events and creating discussion around events or topics that already interest people is a great way to generate awareness and draw members to your group.
- Stay relevant: Keep up to date with new developments.
- Let the good times roll: Hold a social event that your group or organization sponsors to let people have a good time while getting the word out about your activities.

the activities necessary to achieve goals. To be a successful leader one must inspire others to embrace a shared vision. Once they agree on the vision, a leader provides the tools and support that enable team members to achieve it, while encouraging them to ensure success.

QUALITIES OF A LEADER

To be a leader, a person must have personal qualities that make other people want to follow him or her. Among the most

Personal qualities such as supportiveness and effectiveness can inspire others to follow one's lead when a school or work project must be accomplished.

important qualities are self-discipline, organizational ability, empathy, dependability, fair-mindedness, and ethics.

Self-discipline means that a person does what needs to be done, even when no one is forcing him or her to do so. Doing what one should do isn't always fun, but self-discipline pays off in the long run. It makes a person effective and reliable.

Organizational ability means being able to break down tasks into steps that can be performed to accomplish a goal. Often this involves prioritizing tasks and making a schedule indicating what needs to be done to accomplish each task.

The key to making people want to follow you is understanding them. To understand people one needs empathy. Empathy is the ability to put oneself in another person's place, perceiving and feeling things as the other person does. This understanding allows a leader to reassure, encourage, and instruct others effectively.

Dependability, or trustworthiness, is one of the most important qualities of a leader. The members of a team or group must believe that the leader will stand by his or her word. They must believe that the leader is really working for the best interests of the group and can be relied upon to do what is best for everyone, not just serve his or her own self-interest.

Chapter 2

COMMUNICATION IS EVERYTHING

Communication is the cornerstone of leadership. Leaders must motivate their followers by conveying verbally and in writing the vision, goals, tasks, and accomplishments of the group. Leaders must communicate with superiors, subordinates, peers, community leaders, and others. There are many elements to communication. Verbal communication, body language, and attitude are all important in communication.

THE POWER OF WORDS

To communicate well one must organize ideas and present them effectively. Good communication is well planned, clear, easy to follow, and to the point. First it is necessary to understand who the audience is. You would communicate differently when conferring with school officials than you would when asking local businesspeople for donations, talking to fellow students, or addressing potential customers, for example. Who the audience is will affect the language you use and how formally you speak. No matter whom you are speaking to, your grammar should be correct, and

Leaders are often expected to be adept public speakers. Learning to communicate clearly and effectively allows one to engage and persuade others.

you should avoid using slang and jargon (language shared only by a specific group of people). Using correct grammar helps ensure that the message is clearly understood. Before making a presentation, it is a good idea to outline the key points. Doing so allows one to present material in a coherent and organized fashion.

When making a presentation or meeting with people whose help the group needs, it is important to dress neatly and behave in a respectful, polite manner. Looking and acting professional make other people take you seriously.

Body language can be as important as what one says. Facial expressions, posture, and gestures are all part of body language.

People react more positively to those who appear open, relaxed, and friendly. Having good posture and looking people in the eye when speaking make you appear more confident. Maintaining eye contact also helps keep people focused on you.

LISTENING IS MORE THAN HEARING

Often what a leader hears is just as important as what he or she says. People want a leader who will listen to them and who they feel understands their concerns. A leader who listens well will hear about and understand issues that come up, which allows him or her to address problems before they become major obstacles.

Good listening techniques must be learned, and they require practice. A series of techniques called active listening can improve a leader's ability to hear and understand what others are saying. These techniques include the following:

- When someone is speaking, focus on the speaker, not on other things or people in the room. Listen to what he or she is saying, rather than thinking about how you want to respond.
- Make sure the person knows you're listening by nodding or saying something like "right" or "uh-huh."
- Let the speaker finish speaking before you start to talk.
- Summarize what the speaker has said, to make sure that you have understood correctly. If you're not sure what the speaker meant, ask questions.
- If you disagree with the speaker, respond respectfully. Be honest, but do not respond in a way that is offensive to the speaker. Responding in an angry or abusive way will make

The ability to listen to others is a major factor in understanding other people and encouraging their commitment. Developing good listening skills is critical for a leader.

other people see you in a negative way and lead them to be less open with you.

ELECTRONIC ETIQUETTE

Texting, live chat, and social networking have made electronic communication a large part of the way people communicate. Today, communication with the members of a group often takes place through electronic media, such as e-mail, and social media, such as Twitter and Facebook. When you communicate via electronic means, what you send is often available for access or retransmission by other people, some of whom may not be the intended recipients. Much as with a television broadcast, one must assume that everyone in the world can see the communication. In addition, it is virtually impossible to remove all traces of a communication once it has been transmitted. For this reason, it is very important to be sensitive to the feelings of others, both the members of the group and those outside the group, when communicating electronically. Your image as a person and a leader will be affected by what you post or send, so think carefully about what you say before you communicate via electronic means. Moreover, you should follow the same rules for communicating effectively and conveying respect that you would follow in verbal or print communications.

WRITING EFFECTIVELY

Written communication plays a key role in the success of most projects. From proposals to gain permission or funds for a project to press releases to inform the public about the group's activities, a leader must do a lot of writing. How effectively one writes determines a group's success. The rules of grammar allow communication to take place clearly and with a minimum of confusion.

THE ROLE OF SOCIAL MEDIA IN STUDENT LEADERSHIP

Today's students and young workers have grown up in a connected world. They communicate naturally through mobile devices. Therefore, it is necessary for leaders to take advantage of the ways in which social media can be used for effective leadership. The following tips come from the article "Why Social Media Matters for Students in Leadership Roles," on the Localist website.

- Advertising events: Social media offers an effective way for students to advertise their group's events and meetings.
- Intragroup communication, group management, and training: Many students used to ultrafast communication don't bother to read their e-mail, which they find too slow a means of communication. Student leaders can use Twitter hashtags to conduct training or live tweet meetings and have members follow along. They can make quick announcements via YouTube, and members can RSVP to meetings and sign up for events using the online Facebook-integrated calendar.
- Program assessment and feedback: It is vital to assess the impact of a group's event or work. Leaders can collect suggestions and data for evaluation through an online application such as Localist or through Facebook comments or polls.
- Social media ambassadors and community builders: Social media can also offer an opportunity for student leaders to learn how to connect with others and function as community builders.

It is important for a leader to understand the latest forms of online technology and how they can be used to enhance the process of communication among group members.

Therefore, it is important to learn these rules. Take a course in English grammar or read a book on composition, such as *The Elements of Style* by William Strunk Jr. and E. B. White. When preparing written communication, the key is to plan what you want to say before beginning to write. First create an outline of the material to be covered. To keep communication clear, express one idea per paragraph. Make sure that what is being communicated is clear and specific. Some people feel that using big words and complicated phrasing makes them sound smart, but in reality, it is more important that people understand what the leader wants them to do. That goal is often better accomplished

A leader must write many types of communication—from e-mails to reports. Understanding the rules for effective writing minimizes confusion and increases the persuasiveness of one's message.

by means of simple words and straightforward language.

All written material should be proofread by the writer or another person. Typos and mistakes in written communications make you look sloppy and unprofessional. You can't rely on a spell checker. It will not find mistakes such as missing words or homonyms (words that sound alike but have different spellings and meanings, such as "whole" and "hole"). Nor will it catch instances where the writer typed the wrong word, such as "not" instead of "now," because the incorrect word is spelled correctly.

Following the rules for effective communication can allow one to more effectively influence people and achieve a group's goals.

Chapter 3

THE FUTURE AND HOW TO GET THERE

In order to lead one must have a destination. That destination is captured in the leader's vision. A vision is the ultimate result to be achieved. To make a vision into reality, a leader must know how to break down a project into individual goals that can be accomplished.

HAVING A VISION

A vision is a major goal—something large in scale or significance, such as winning the state basketball championship, creating a park for underprivileged children, or getting a candidate elected to public office. The key aspect of a vision is that it is greater than what can be achieved by one person alone. It must inspire others, making them feel they are working toward something important.

All great leaders have a compelling vision of how things could be. The vision makes it clear what the group is trying to achieve and makes people want to rise to the challenge and work enthusiastically toward a goal. A compelling vision also holds the group together and keeps them focused when obstacles arise.

A leader must have a vision of what might be in order to convince others that there is a goal that is worth working toward and to keep them contributing.

GETTING PEOPLE TO BUY IN

Once a leader has established a goal, the next step is to get people to work toward achieving it. To get people to buy in to the vision, the leader must communicate it in a way that attracts, excites, and challenges people. A vital element in successfully communicating a vision is passion. Therefore, success is more likely when the vision is something the leader believes in strongly.

In order to get people to commit to a project, a leader must understand what motivates people. Some people are excited by the

Volleyball players hold a bake sale to raise money for their team. A leader understands how to make team members feel enthusiastic about working together to accomplish a goal.

chance to accomplish something important. They will respond well to the challenge of the project. Some people are affected by how others see them. They will work to achieve a vision if they think it will enhance their image and make them look good to others. Still other people enjoy the social aspects of a project and will work on it if they find it interesting or fun or if it allows them to work with people they like or admire. The leader must identify what motivates different people and convince them of the benefits of working on the project. At the same time, the leader must be careful not to allow motivating people to turn into manipulation. Manipulation occurs when a leader plays on people's insecurities or fears to get them to do what the leader wants. Manipulating people is unethical and doing so will hurt a leader's reputation.

ESTABLISHING GOALS

To achieve the result described in the vision, one must accomplish many steps along the way. The leader must be able to break down a project into individual goals that can be accomplished by the team. Accomplishing such goals along the way keeps a team energized and focused. Having specific goals makes it possible for the leader and the team to measure their progress. Most projects require a combination of long-term and short-term goals. For example, a long-range goal might be to raise $500 for the local Boys and Girls Club by the end of the year. A short-range goal would be to run a successful bake sale to raise money toward this goal.

It is important to involve the members of the group in creating goals. If the members of a team contribute to establishing the goals, they will be more invested in accomplishing them. Therefore, it is important to get group members to contribute ideas and to use those ideas when establishing goals. Not only will this make team members feel that the goals are theirs, but the group may come up with good ideas that the leader has not thought of. Even though the

EXAMPLES OF SUCCESSFUL STUDENT LEADERSHIP

There are many ways to be a student leader. Examples of student leadership include:

- Holding a class office such as class president or vice president
- Organizing or helping organize a charity event, such as a race in which runners' sponsors donate to the charity or holding a charity car wash
- Helping organize a rally for a good cause such as saving the environment
- Organizing or running a student chapter of a nonprofit organization, such as the Sierra Club
- Organizing a community project, such as getting other students to help clean up a local playground or decorate and furnish a playroom for the children's ward of the local hospital.
- Campaigning for a political candidate
- Organizing a group of students to provide tutoring to their peers or to help younger children learn to read
- Organizing a social event, such as a dance marathon; if the event has a fee, donate what is left after expenses to a local charity

The following are some comments by one student leader to questions about student leadership, which come from the University of California, Davis, Student Leader Profiles website (http://csi.ucdavis.edu/leadership/student-leader-profiles):

Tamara Enriquez, MEDLIFE chapter founder and president, among other positions:

Why do you choose to be involved as a student leader?

I'm very passionate about the purposes of the organizations with which I'm involved. Being a leader is a way to make ideas happen, so the organization progresses in a positive direction.

What have you learned about leadership through your work with others on campus?

Being a leader is a never-ending learning process. You constantly learn about yourself, the people with whom you work, and what works and what doesn't . . . There is an added responsibility in your life, and you must be able to make the correct and ethical decisions even though they may be unpopular. Most important, you must learn how to inspire the entire body of your organization toward a common goal. It's a very dynamic position that tests your character and gives you the opportunity to understand the difference between leadership and management.

whole team may be involved in setting goals, it is ultimately still the leader's responsibility to see that the goals are met.

ASSIGNING TASKS

After goals are established, a leader must set the series of tasks that will allow each goal to be accomplished. The leader then assigns people and resources to each task. The key to getting tasks accomplished is to assign the right people to each one. To do so, the leader must evaluate the members' individual skills and talents. People have different skills, talents, and abilities. Some people have more knowledge than others about subjects such as math, computers, or

Students prepare posters for a fund-raiser. A leader assigns tasks that best use each person's skills—in this case making the most of their artistic talents.

languages. Some are more artistic. Some are better athletes or have better mechanical skills. However, all people have abilities that a

leader can use. In any project there are a variety of tasks that must be carried out. Evaluating the skills, knowledge, and experience of team members allows a leader to assign each person to tasks he or she can do well. This way everyone can make a contribution and feel a sense of accomplishment. A true leader helps weaker members improve their skills and make a contribution, rather than belittling them. He or she insists that all team members treat each other with respect.

Leaders frequently feel they can execute tasks better than everyone else. It is a mistake, however, to micromanage people. People will follow a leader more readily and work harder if they feel the leader trusts them. A leader demonstrates trust by allowing others to do the tasks assigned to them without constantly checking on the details of what they're doing. It's better to set up regular times to meet individually or as a group to review the progress that is being made. During such meetings a leader can address any problems and give people assistance or advice. That said, it's important to let team members know they can come to the leader any time they feel they need help or have a problem. This approach puts control of the task in the team members' hands, and such empowerment makes people more willing and eager to work.

Sometimes problems will arise. When issues come up, it is important not to blame them on particular people or allow others to do so. If people feel they won't be blamed, they will be more

When a team member does a good job, it is important to acknowledge that person's contribution and to show appreciation, giving the person a sense of accomplishment.

likely to bring up problems sooner, which will provide more time to solve them. A more effective approach would be to treat problems and mistakes as something the team needs to fix together. The leader needs to emphasize that the success of the project and the team depends on working together to resolve the issue.

It is also important for the leader to let team members know that he or she values their contributions. Therefore, when people accomplish their tasks, the leader should tell them they've done a good job and their efforts are appreciated.

Chapter 4

LEADING A GROUP

Leading a group requires excellent people skills. The material here covers how to get a team composed of individuals to work together and how to get them to accomplish the goals necessary for a project to succeed. Leaders must be able to keep a group together, even when a project encounters an obstacle, or the leader must make an unpopular decision. Sooner or later the leader will have to deal with conflict within the group and still be able keep the group working toward its goals. The first step is to forge a team from the individuals involved.

TEAM BUILDING

At school and in the workplace, competitiveness and individual achievement are often emphasized. However, for a group to be successful, the leader must get members to put aside their individual desire for recognition and to work for the good of the group as a whole. One way to encourage the group to work together is to remind the group, at the start of each meeting or event, of the goal it is trying to achieve. Keeping the focus on the vision they are trying to achieve helps get members' attention off themselves.

However, there is no denying that people desire recognition. The leader can encourage team building by recognizing and praising those who demonstrate desirable behavior, rather than just those who accomplish something on their own. For example, reward those who are outstanding when they help other team members, which contributes to the group's success, not just their own. This will make the stars more likely to help the team as a whole, because they know they will receive recognition for doing so. At the same time, other members will benefit from the opportunity to improve their skills.

The leader should thank every person for doing the task he or she was assigned. This makes everyone feel valued, and it helps reduce competition for attention among team members. Providing a social element to group work can also help people relax and become friendly. For example, one might order pizza for the group while it is working on a project.

BRINGING PEOPLE TOGETHER

One of the hardest but most rewarding tasks of a leader is bringing together people of diverse backgrounds, cultures, and economic

Having people with different backgrounds and experiences can make a team stronger because there is a wider range of knowledge to draw on. Everyone should feel welcome to contribute.

classes. People who join groups or are assigned to work on teams have had different experiences and have different types of

MENTORING

Mentoring is a process whereby an experienced individual assists a less experienced person to develop his or her skills by providing one-on-one guidance. Having a mentor can help a new leader develop leadership skills faster and avoid mistakes. A mentor can also provide advice when a young leader is faced with a difficult situation. In business, a mentor is often a more experienced manager who takes a promising young manager under his or her wing. In school, a mentor might be a coach, a teacher, a guidance counselor, or a professional in a field a student is interested in. The mentor might even be an older family member or family friend. The first step in locating a mentor is to identify a person whose leadership skills you respect. Explain that you admire the person's leadership ability. Tell him or her that you are leading a group or team, and ask if he or she would be willing to advise you. If the person can't mentor you because of other commitments, ask if he or she can recommend someone else, or ask another person you admire.

If the person agrees, talk to him or her regularly, either face-to-face or via e-mail. Discuss your activities and any issues you face. Your mentor will be able to give you much valuable advice. However, although your mentor has gained knowledge over time, everyone's situation is unique. Be sure to evaluate your mentor's suggestions, and decide if each is appropriate for the situation. The goal of having a mentor is developing the ability to manage on your own. Feel free to share with your mentor what worked and what didn't. However, it is important to show gratitude to your mentor and thank him or her for the help.

A mentor helps a student. A mentor can provide insight into how to approach a project or solve a problem based on his or her experience with similar issues and more extensive knowledge.

personalities. The leader is responsible for making sure everyone feels comfortable contributing.

An important element is creating an environment where everyone feels free to express their ideas. When ideas are discussed, the leader must make sure everyone has a chance to speak. An important part of this exchange is keeping members from shouting down other people's ideas before they've had their chance to express them fully. If necessary, the leader should ask those who are reluctant to speak to share their ideas. The leader must insist that group members treat each other with respect. Stronger members must not be allowed to bully weak ones, and no one should be allowed to pick on people who are different.

TO DO OR NOT TO DO?

One of the most important elements of effective leadership is decision making. Mastering decision making isn't easy. A leader needs to be decisive, but also remain flexible enough to adjust decisions when conditions change. Thus, leadership requires a balance between decisiveness and flexibility. In order to get tasks done and achieve goals, a leader must be able to make decisions even without having complete information or knowing the perfect solution. Indecisiveness—not being able to make a decision or constantly changing course—is one of the biggest inhibitors of success.

One reason for indecision is perfectionism, believing that one must have the best possible solution. A leader must find a way to get each job done well and each problem solved, even if the approach chosen isn't the perfect answer. Doing nothing for long periods of time because one is constantly searching for the perfect answer will interfere with getting the project done or the problem solved in a timely fashion. One should look for a solution that will successfully accomplish the task or goal. A leader must be decisive. He or she must be willing to make a choice among possible courses of action arrived at by the group and then stick to that choice—unless the situation itself changes. However, a leader must also recognize that sometimes situations change, or new facts come to light that affect the assumptions the original plan was based on. A good leader recognizes when new information or events legitimately require a change of plan. By assessing the group's progress at regular points, a leader can judge whether the present course is still correct or needs to be adjusted. A good leader acknowledges when he or she has made a mistake. Stubbornly refusing to admit one is wrong and adjust one's course when appropriate can lead to disaster.

FOSTERING CREATIVITY

A leader needs the group members to come up with creative ideas on how to accomplish tasks, solve problems, and achieve goals. To encourage creativity one needs to establish an atmosphere in which team members can express their ideas without being criticized or judged. It is often difficult to get people to accept new ideas. It is up to the leader to see that new ideas that might be beneficial get a fair hearing. The leader must insist that members hear what each person has to say before criticizing the idea or coming up with objections.

A practical way to encourage creativity is simply to let people take responsibility for how to perform their tasks. A leader tells people what their tasks are but doesn't insist that things be done his or her way. Instead, the leader lets people come up with their own methods. This approach can result in improvements in the way things are done. Similarly, if a problem arises, a leader should give the person responsibility for the task or give the whole team a chance to develop ways to solve the problem before stepping in. If people do come up with solutions to a problem, the leader should acknowledge their contributions.

Brainstorming is a technique often used to foster creativity. This is a handy technique to get the members of a group to come up with creative ideas. In brainstorming, one wants to have as many members of the group present as possible, so there are people with many different points of view. The leader states the issue or problem as an open-ended question. For example, "How can we renovate the community playground?" Next, the leader sets a number or time

Creating an atmosphere in which team members can express their ideas and make suggestions without being criticized encourages them to contribute and be creative.

limit, such as collecting fifty ideas or all the ideas possible in half an hour. The group members then write down their ideas or call them out. When the limit is reached, the leader writes the ideas on a flip chart, whiteboard, or blackboard so that everyone can see them. No one should be allowed to make comments about the ideas, no matter how silly they may seem. Next, a list of judging criteria is established, such as: the group must be able to raise enough money to pay for it; it must comply with school, company, or government regulations; it must be achievable over summer vacation or by the end of the year; it must be safe; and so on.

The pros and cons of each idea are then discussed. If there are too many ideas to discuss all of them, the leader can have each group member give each idea a score from zero to five, and then the group can discuss the top five or ten ideas. Finally, the best idea or ideas are chosen by the group. The leader may get consensus (general agreement) from the group, or members may vote on which idea they prefer; alternately, they may give each idea a score from zero to five, and the ideas can then be ranked from most to least preferred. The most popular ideas can then be explored further.

CONFLICT

There are many types of conflict that can occur within a group, and the leader must be able to deal with them. Issues include team members dominating

When conflict arises, a leader must be able to get team members to address their differences in a constructive, not destructive, manner.

or intimidating other teams members, people who are toxically negative, and arguments and confrontations.

Sometimes one of the members of a team will be extremely negative. This person will constantly point out why everything suggested will not work and why everything done isn't good enough. This attitude can demoralize the entire group. The leader must neutralize this person before his or her toxic attitude poisons the entire project. One way to do this is by counteracting the negative viewpoint. Acknowledge that what he or she says might—or might not—turn out to be true, then ask for a positive idea about the plan or task. If the person won't respond positively, ask other members of the group what they think is positive.

Confrontations occur when one person starts picking on another, or two people begin arguing. It's best to stop such confrontations right away, before they get out of control. If two people start trading nasty remarks, the leader can say something like, "Come on, guys, let's focus on what we're all trying to do here and not get personal." The leader should remind people that they all agreed they would treat each other with respect. Often, a leader can use humor to defuse a tense situation. It's important not to make fun of the people in the confrontation, however. If there appears to be a real problem, a leader will take the people involved to a separate room and discuss the problem with them, listening to both sides of the story and helping the two people arrive at a solution.

It's critical not to get between two people who are engaged in a confrontation. Doing so could be dangerous if the confrontation turns physical. If it looks as if the people involved might become violent, it is best to get help. In school this might mean finding a teacher or other authority. At work it might mean contacting security. If it appears that there is a danger of violence, the leader should have everyone else leave the room or area. Sometimes, simply having everyone walk out causes those having the confrontation to stop.

Although there is no one way to deal with all problem people, one of the most successful approaches is to redirect them from being disruptive to being constructive. Often disruptive people feel insecure. They crave attention and want to feel important. Ask them to help with the group, a task, or solving a problem. Making them feel important can often turn them from troublemakers to people who want "their" project to succeed.

Chapter 5

BEING A TRUE LEADER

The most effective method of leadership is leading by example. The behavior of the leader determines the behavior of team members. Therefore, how a leader behaves personally and professionally, including being trustworthy and ethical, determines how group or team members will behave.

DO WHAT I DO

What a person does creates a much stronger impression than what he or she says. True leaders inspire admiration and a desire to emulate them. It is important to behave in a way that encourages others to follow that example. There is no such thing as "do as I say, not as I do" when it comes to leadership. No matter what the leader says, group members will pattern their behavior on what the leader does. Therefore, a leader who wants people to work hard, be respectful toward each other, and put the team first must do so as well. If the leader doesn't behave in the way he or says is appropriate, group or team members will simply think, "Why should I behave that way, if the leader doesn't?"

BE TRUE TO YOURSELF AND OTHERS

True leaders have integrity. Integrity means being true to yourself and what you believe in. A leader with integrity stands up for what is right and behaves in an honorable manner, even in situations where this is difficult. The single most important element in gaining and keeping followers is trust. People will join a group or team if they trust the person leading it. If they find out the leader is not trustworthy, they will abandon the group. If they have to work with an untrustworthy person on a team at school or work, they will do so reluctantly, putting out minimal effort because they do not believe what the leader says. Make no mistake: with cell phones that take photos and video and social media applications like Facebook and Twitter, if a leader behaves badly, people will find out.

What makes a leader trustworthy? One aspect is a willingness to do what is right rather than what is popular. Refusing to go along with bullying when one's friends do it, and insisting that they stop, is one example. Another is not taking credit for the achievements of the group but insisting that praise be shared. A third aspect is not cheating. Whether it's cheating on a test at school or lying on an expense account at work, if a person cheats in one way, people will assume that person might cheat them, too.

On the positive side, when a leader behaves honestly and does what's right, group or team members see that person as someone who can be relied upon and who will defend them when necessary and as someone who looks out for the best interests of group members and the team as a whole—in short, a leader.

Being ethical and insisting that team members behave ethically as well earns respect for both the leader and the team.

BUILDING TRUST

How does one build trust? A leader asks the group to put the group's interests before their own. A leader must be prepared to do the same. Making sure that group members get credit for the group's accomplishments is one of the best ways to gain members' trust. Nothing will destroy trust in the leader faster than taking credit for the group's accomplishments. The leader may be the one who creates the vision and plan. He or she may direct the activities of the group. Nonetheless, when the time comes to distribute credit, a leader makes it clear to others that it was people in the group who were responsible for the project's success. Receiving recognition makes people feel valued and gives them a sense of satisfaction and accomplishment. Leaders who see that group members receive recognition make people trust them and want to follow them. This also makes people likely to work harder for the group in the future.

MEETING THE CHALLENGE

The only real way to learn leadership is through practical experience. To become a leader, one must put oneself out front and take

A successful leader acknowledges team members' contributions to the success of a project, which helps increase their future commitment.

charge of a project, group, or team. This can be a scary prospect. One of the key elements of leadership is self-confidence. If people

FAILING IS THE BEGINNING OF SUCCESS

Dealing with failure is not easy, but it is a skill that is necessary to learn if one wants to be a successful leader. Karen Finerman is chief executive officer of the investment firm Metropolitan Capital Management and a regular on CNBC's TV show *Fast Money*. In her book, *Finerman's Rules: Secrets I'd Only Tell My Daughters About Business and Life*, she has this to say about failure:

"This is the moment on which success is built—not the victories, the winning, the momentum or the luck. It is in this moment you will decide what you are made of and what your character truly is."

The following is a an excellent series of steps for recovering from failure, taken from her book:

"1. Fake it—play hurt and get back in the game.

2. Plot your future—set incremental, achievable goals.

3. Recalibrate—get a fresh view and perspective.

4. Change it up—do daily things that give you a fresh start."

The important thing about failure is not to let it stop you from trying again. Learning from your mistakes can make you successful the next time around.

don't believe in themselves, neither will others. People learn by believing that they have or can learn the skills necessary to meet the challenges of leadership. No leader has the solution to every problem. However, leaders know they are capable of dealing with questions and problems. When problems arise, people rely on the leader to remain calm and direct them toward a solution. The leader must see that members of the group cooperate in an orderly manner and keep them from panicking. This ability is one reason that people see the leader as a strong and secure person who can be depended upon.

It is important to understand that confidence is not arrogance. Confidence is knowing one can deal with things. Arrogance is flaunting one's knowledge or skill. Constantly stating or demonstrating how smart or skilled one is merely makes other people feel inferior or resentful. These feelings make them want to stay away from the leader and not follow him or her. Therefore, it is better to show your confidence through what you do, rather than by talking about how much you know or how skilled you are.

How does one gain confidence? By taking on challenges. Seeing a challenge through to the end gives you a chance to experience and learn all aspects of leadership. Whenever you plan to accomplish a goal, there are likely to be obstacles. Sometimes you will fail. Along the way, however, you will gain experience in how to handle the problems and issues that arise. The result is knowing that you can deal with problems and that you can survive the challenges of leadership. It is not necessary to succeed in every challenge. Most successful leaders have failed somewhere along the way. Indeed, successful people feel that if they never fail, they are not challenging themselves enough. These people understand that the ability to fail and then try again is the type of self-confidence that defines a leader.

LEARNING NEVER ENDS

The better and broader a leader's skills are, the more effective he or she will be. While in high school and college one can lay a foundation by taking courses in a variety of subjects, not just those related to the career field one chooses. Taking courses in literature,

Students share what they've learned in a cultural leadership program. Learning about history and other cultures fosters an understanding that is helpful, especially in today's global economy.

history, and other fields in the humanities can give you an understanding of other people's cultures, which helps when dealing with people from varied backgrounds. Courses in English grammar, writing, and public speaking improve your communication skills. In college, areas worth studying include fund-raising, public speaking, composition, project planning, and accounting and financial management, among others. It is also useful to have good computer skills.

Being a leader means keeping your academic, professional, and leadership skills up to date in a world where information and technology are constantly changing. This means that learning does not end when a person leaves school. It is necessary to learn new tools and techniques as they are developed. One way to gain information on leadership tools and techniques is by reading print or online magazines on management. Another is to join professional organizations such as the American Management Association and industry-specific organizations in one's field. These organizations offer the opportunity to attend conferences and workshops and often provide print or online resources. They provide an excellent opportunity to learn from others' experiences. Before adopting a management technique, however, one needs to critically evaluate it to make sure it is actually useful and not just a fad and to make sure it is appropriate and ethical.

For a leader, learning doesn't end with new leadership techniques. Being a great leader requires having knowledge of many subjects. When leading a group, generating ideas, and solving problems, it is beneficial to have a wide range of expertise. History, literature, mathematics, science, psychology, languages, the arts, and other subjects can all provide information of use to a leader. A broad spectrum of knowledge allows a leader to view a problem from a variety of perspectives, which often results in solutions that are not seen by people with a narrower training. Continuing to learn throughout your life is one of the keys to success. Successful leaders are always seeking more knowledge and more experience.

GLOSSARY

active listening A method of attending to what others say that ensures one hears and understands their meaning.

articulate Capable of communicating in a clear and well-organized way.

bias Prejudice in favor of or against one thing, person, or group compared with another, usually in a way considered to be unfair.

coherent Organized in a way that makes sense.

consensus Agreement among a group of people.

constructive Productive, useful.

dedication A strong commitment.

divisive Causing disunity.

emulate To model oneself after, or try to be like.

endeavor An undertaking.

globalization A process in which business extends all over the world.

homonyms Words that sound the same but have different meanings, such as "bear" and "bare."

inhibitor Something that blocks or slows something else.

integrity The quality of being true to one's beliefs; the quality of being honest and honorable.

jargon Terms used by a particular group that may not be understood by those outside the group.

legitimate True to established principals.

micromanage To tell people how to do the details of their job.

motivate To inspire.

persevere To persist or stay on a course of action despite obstacles.

routine Regular or customary.

FOR MORE INFORMATION

American Management Association (AMA)
1601 Broadway
New York, NY 10019
(212) 586-8100
Website: http://www.amanet.org
The AMA offers books, seminars, and other resources on management. It also offers student membership.

J-Teen Leadership
701 Westchester Avenue, Suite 203E
White Plains, NY 10604
(914) 328-8788
Website: http://www.jteenleadership.org
The J-Teen Leadership organization empowers Jewish teens from all backgrounds with leadership training.

Kiwanis Key-Leader
3636 Woodview Trace
Indianapolis, IN 46268
(800) 549-2647, ext. 124
Website: http://www.key-leader.org
Kiwanis Key-Leader is a program of Kiwanis International that offers leadership resources and programs for teens.

National 4-H Council
7100 Connecticut Avenue
Chevy Chase, MD 20815
(301) 961-2800
Website: http://www.4-h.org

The National 4-H Council offers a variety of resources and programs to develop practical skills and leadership capabilities in young people.

National Teen Leadership Program
101 Parkshore Drive
Folsom, CA 95630
(800) 550-1950
Website: http://www.ntlp.org
The National Teen Leadership Program provides leadership programs for teens, including summer and one-day programs.

Teen Leadership Corps
26 E. Cedar Point Road
Sandusky, OH 44870
(419) 621-5426
Website: http://www.teenleadershipcorps.com
The Teen Leadership Corps provides opportunities for teens to learn leadership skills through involvement in community service.

Teen Leadership Foundation
1280 Bison Avenue, B9-115
Newport Beach, CA 92660
(949) 769-6670
Website: http://www.teenleadershipfoundation.org
The Teen Leadership Foundation provides leadership programs for teens who are in the foster care system or being aged out of it. It also circulates an e-mail newsletter.

Youth in Motion
245 Eglinton Avenue East, Suite 303
Toronto, ON M4P 0B3

Canada
(416) 962-4946
Website: http://www.youth-in-motion.ca
Youth in Motion is a nonprofit organization whose goal is to provide engaging, inspiring, and educational programs for youth to assist them in succeeding in a rewarding career path. It sponsors the Top 20 Under 20 program, which honors the top twenty student leaders from across Canada.

Youth Leadership Camps Canada
498 Moon Point Drive
Orillia, ON L3V 6H1
Canada
(705) 326-2433
Website: http://www.ylcc.com
Youth Leadership Camps Canada is an organization that provides leadership training programs for teens who want to develop their leadership skills.

WEBSITES

Due to the changing nature of Internet links, Rosen Publishing has developed an online list of websites related to the subject of this book. This site is updated regularly. Please use this link to access the list:

http://www.rosenlinks.com/WAWR/Lead

FOR FURTHER READING

Blanchard, Ken, Patricia Zigarmi, and Drea Zigarmi. *Leadership and the One Minute Manager: Increasing Effectiveness Through Situational Leadership II*. New York, NY: HarperCollins, 2013.

Bradberry, Travis, Jean Greaves, and Patrick M. Lencioni. *Emotional Intelligence 2.0*. San Diego, CA: TalentSmart, 2009.

Facts On File, Inc. *Communication Skills* (Career Skills Library). New York, NY: Infobase Publishing, 2009.

Finerman, Karen. *Finerman's Rules: Secrets I'd Only Tell My Daughters About Business and Life*. New York, NY: Grand Central Press, 2013.

Hackman, Michael Z., and Craig E. Johnson. *Leadership: A Communication Perspective*. Sixth edition. Long Grove, IL: Waveland Press, 2013.

Jennings, Jason. *Hit the Ground Running: A Manual for New Leaders*. New York, NY: Penguin, 2009.

Kahaner, Ellen. *Great Communication Skills* (Work Readiness). New York, NY: Rosen Publishing, 2008.

Kouzes, James M., and Barry Z. Posner. *The Student Leadership Challenge: Five Practices for Exemplary Leaders*. San Francisco, CA: Jossey-Bass, 2008.

Kouzes, James M., and Barry Z. Posner. *The Truth About Leadership: The No-Fads, Heart-of-the-Matter Facts You Need to Know*. San Francisco, CA: Jossey-Bass, 2010.

MacKay, Matthew, Martha Davis, and Patrick Fanning. *Messages: The Communication Skills Book*. Oakland, CA: New Harbinger Publications, 2009.

McCollum, Sean, and Madonna M. Murphy. *Managing Conflict Resolution*. New York, NY: Chelsea House Publishers, 2009.

Miller, Mark. *The Heart of Leadership: Becoming a Leader People Want to Follow.* San Francisco, CA: Berrett-Koehler Publishers, 2013.

Nelson, Bob, and Peter Economy. *Managing for Dummies.* Hoboken, NJ: Wiley Publishing, 2010.

Rath, Tom, and Barry Conchie. *Strengths-Based Leadership: Great Leaders, Teams, and Why People Follow.* New York, NY: Gallup Press, 2009.

Shankman, Marcy L., and Scott J. Allen. *Emotionally Intelligent Leadership for Students: Development Guide.* San Francisco, CA: Jossey-Bass, 2010.

Snyder, Steven. *Leadership and the Art of Struggle: How Great Leaders Grow through Challenge and Adversity.* San Francisco, CA: Berrett-Koehler, 2013.

Sommers, Michael. *Great Interpersonal Skills* (Work Readiness). New York, NY: Rosen Publishing, 2008.

Sprenger, B. Marilee. *The Leadership Brain for Dummies.* Hoboken, NJ: Wiley Publishing, 2010.

Thelen, Tom. *Teen Leadership Revolution: How Ordinary Teens Become Extraordinary Leaders.* Grand Rapids, MI: CharacterPrograms.org, 2012.

BIBLIOGRAPHY

All Business/Div. D&B. "Ten Ways to Improve Your Interpersonal Skills." Retrieved October 2, 2013 (http://www.allbusiness.com/human-resources/careers-career-development/11134-1.html).

Baumgartner, Jeffrey. "The Step-by-Step Guide to Brainstorming." JPD.com. Retrieved October 4, 2013 (http://www.jpb.com/creative/brainstorming.php).

Burns, Karen. "On Careers: 13 Tips for Finding a Mentor." *U.S. News*, January 13, 2010. Retrieved October 3, 2013 (http://money.usnews.com/money/blogs/outside-voices-careers/2010/01/13/13-tips-on-finding-a-mentor).

Finerman, Karen. *Finerman's Rules: Secrets I'd Only Tell My Daughters About Business and Life*. New York, NY: Grand Central Publishing, 2013.

Free Management Library. "All About Teambuilding." Retrieved October 2, 2013 (http://managementhelp.org/grp_skll/teams/teams.htm).

Global Zero. "Tips for Student Leaders." Retrieved October 24, 2013 (http://www.globalzero.org/files/gz_tips_from_student_leaders_0213.pdf).

Inc.com. "Better Communication with Employees and Peers." Retrieved September 28, 2013 (http://www.inc.com/guides/growth/23032.html).

Learning Center. "How to Build a Team." Retrieved October 7, 2013 (http://www.learningcenter.net/library/building.shtml).

LocalList. "Why Social Media Matters for Students in Leadership Roles." Retrieved October 23, 2013 (http://blog.localist.com/post/30451610798/why-social-media-matters-for-students-in-leadership).

Kouzes, James M., and Barry Z. Posner. *The Truth about Leadership.* San Francisco, CA; Jossey-Bass, 2010.

Maxell, John. *Teamwork 101.* Nashville, TN: Maxwell Motivation, 2009.

MindTools. "Active Listening." Retrieved September 28, 2013 (http://www.mindtools.com/CommSkll/ActiveListening.htm).

MindTools. "Conflict Resolution." Retrieved October 2, 2013 (http://www.mindtools.com/pages/article/newLDR_81.htm).

Rye, David. *Stop Managing and Lead.* Avon, MA: Adams Press, 2009.

University of California, Davis. "Student Leader Profiles." Retrieved October 26, 2013 (http://csi.ucdavis.edu/leadership/student-leader-profiles).

INDEX

ABOUT THE AUTHOR

Jeri Freedman has a B.A. from Harvard University. She is the author of numerous young adult nonfiction books, many published by Rosen Publishing, including *First Bank Account and First Investments*, *Careers in Human Resources*, *The U.S. Economic Crisis*, and *Women in the Workplace: Wages, Respect, and Equal Rights*.

PHOTO CREDITS

Cover Mandy Godbehear/Shutterstock.com; p. 5 © Jeff Greenberg/Alamy; p. 7 The Washington Post/Getty Images; pp. 8–9, 14 Jupiterimages/Photos.com/Thinkstock; p. 11 Dr. Heinz Linke/iStock/Thinkstock; p. 16 Helder Almeida/iStock/Thinkstock; p. 19 Monkey Business/Thinkstock; pp. 20-21 Don Bayley/iStock/Thinkstock; p. 23 Yellow Dog Productions/Photodisc/Getty Images; p. 24 © Bob Daemmrich/The Image Works; pp. 28–29, 35, 50–51 © AP Images; p. 30 LittleBee80/iStock/Thinkstock; pp. 32–33 LuckyBusiness/iStock/Thinkstock; pp. 38–39 Stockbyte/Thinkstock; pp. 40-41 Medioimages/Photodisc/Thinkstock; p. 45 The Boston Globe/Getty Images; pp. 46–47 Cultura/Lilly Bloom/Riser/Getty Images; cover and interior graphic elements Artens/Shutterstock.com (figures, urban environment), LeksusTuss/Shutterstock.com (abstract patterns).

Designer: Brian Garvey; Editor: Shalini Saxena;
Photo Researcher: Amy Feinberg